The Last Trip to Oron

The Spirals Series

Plays

Jan Carew
Computer Killer

Chris Culshaw
Dribs and Drabs
Gaffs and Laughs
Radio Riff-Raff

Christine Dawe
The Wanna Beez

Julia Donaldson
Books and Crooks

Nigel Gray
An Earwig in the Ear

Angela Griffiths
TV Hospital
Wally and Co

Paul Groves
Tell Me Where it Hurts

Julia Pattison
Kicking Up a Stink

Bill Ridgway
Monkey Business

John Townsend
A Bit of a Shambles
Cheer and Groan
Chef's Night Off
Clogging the Works
Cowboys, Jelly and Custard
Gulp and Gasp
Hiccups and Slip-ups
Jumping the Gun
A Lot of Old Codswallop
A Maggot in the Mouthwash
Murder at Muckleby Manor

David Walke
The Good, the Bad and the Bungle
Package Holiday

Non-fiction

Jim Alderson
Crash in the Jungle

Jan Carew
Eyam, Plague Village

Chris Culshaw
Dive into Danger
Ground Zero

David Orme
Hackers

Jill Ridge
Lifelines

Bill Ridgway
Break Out!
Lost in Alaska
Over the Wall
A Soldiers Tale

Julie Taylor
Lucky Dip

John Townsend
Burke and Hare: The Body Snatchers
Kingdom of the Man-eaters
Raiders of the Dome Diamond
Trapped Under Ground

Keith West
Back to the Wild
The Great Trek

Fiction

Jim Alderson
The Witch Princess

Penny Bates
Tiger of the Lake

Jan Carew
Footprints in the Sand
Voices in the Dark

Susan Duberley
The Ring

John Goodwin
Ghost Train

Angela Griffiths
Diary of a Wild Thing
Stories of Suspense

Anita Jackson
The Actor
The Austin Seven
Bennet Manor
Dreams
The Ear
A Game of Life and Death
No Rent to Pay

Paul Jennings
Eye of Evil
Maggot

Richard Kemble
Grandmother's Secret

Helen Lowerson
The Biz

Margaret Loxton
The Dark Shadow

Bill Ridgway
The Hawkstone
The Last Trip to Oron
The Power of the Hawkstone
Mr Punch
Spots

John Townsend
Back on the Prowl
Beware the Morris Minor
A Minute to Kill
Night Beast
Snow Beast
Sweet Dreams

NEW Spirals   *FICTION*

The Last Trip to Oron

Bill Ridgway

Text © Bill Ridgway 2004

The right of Bill Ridgway to be identified as the author of this work has been asserted by him in accordance with the Copyright, Designs and Patents Act 1988.

All rights reserved. No part of this publication may be reproduced or transmitted in any form or by any means, electronic or mechanical, including photocopy, recording or any information storage and retrieval system, without permission in writing from the publisher or under licence from the Copyright Licensing Agency Limited, 90 Tottenham Court Road, London W1T 4LP.

Any person who commits any unauthorised act in relation to this publication may be liable to criminal prosecution and civil claims for damages.

Published in 2004 by:
Nelson Thornes Ltd
Delta Place
27 Bath Road
CHELTENHAM
GL53 7TH
United Kingdom

04 05 06 07 08 / 10 9 8 7 6 5 4 3 2 1

A catalogue record for this book is available from the British Library

ISBN 0 7487 9001 2

Cover illustration by Paul McCaffrey, c/o Sylvie Poggio Artists Agency
Page make-up by Tech-Set, Gateshead

Printed in Croatia by Zrinski

1

Captain McKenna looked out into deep space. Stars and planets sparked in the blackness. No matter how many times he made the trip, he never tired of the view.

One planet stood out from the rest. Oron. It glowed like a pink bead. McKenna and his crew were heading for it for the last time. His old ship, Galeta, had seen better days.

McKenna was the boss of Oron Mining. He'd set up the company many years ago. At that time there'd been a lot of gold on Oron. Earth had run out, but Oron had plenty. Trips had taken months. It was still worth it. Gold had given him a good life.

But now Oron was nearly mined out too. One more trip to pick up the last load and Oron Mining would be history.

He heard voices. Bella was coming on deck with Dron. Dron was a giant. He came from Korak. He had green, scaly skin like a snake. His heart was on the right side of his body. And he had six fingers on each hand. Apart from that, he was almost human.

Bella was dark and lively. She could out-run a cat, and was just as nimble. The three of them watched the pink planet grow bigger as they drew near.

'Not long now,' McKenna said. 'My last trip.'

'Our last trip,' Dron corrected him.

'My life has been this ship and its cargo,' said McKenna. 'I shall miss it.'

'And Oron?' asked Bella. 'Will you miss Oron?'

McKenna was silent for a moment. Then he said, 'It's given me a living. But I'm not sorry to see the back of it. Oron gave her gold, but I had to fight for every grain.'

Now the planet was spinning under them. 'Time to strap in,' said McKenna. 'Touch down in six minutes.'

There was a roar as the retro-rockets cut in. They waited for the bump. It was a good landing. The motors grew quiet. For a moment they listened to the silence of Oron.

'Better go, Captain,' said Dron.

The hatch hummed open. They stepped down. 'Welcome to the planet of gold,' Mckenna said. 'Let's go and find Ben.'

2

The Oron sun was setting as they got into the pod. Mountains rose sheer into the pink sky. There were no trees, no plants. Nothing but rocky shadows.

'I hope Ben's got us something to eat,' Bella said. 'I'm starving.'

'It's always the same at the end of a trip,' McKenna agreed. 'What do you say, Dron?'

The Korak didn't answer. He was thinking of Ben, the last miner on Oron. Ben had chosen to live alone with just one robot to help him dig for gold.

The sun dipped below the far hills. The sky changed quickly from pink to black. The pod's single beam swept the track. McKenna turned on the heaters.

'Looks like Ben's at home,' he said, pointing to a light in the darkness. They passed a crane and some fuel tanks. The pod's roof slid back. The bitter Oron night hit them like an axe. They ran the few steps to Ben's dome.

Ben wasn't there. Bella called his name. There was no reply. A puzzled look crossed McKenna's face.

'It's not like Ben to play games. He's never away at touchdown. He knew we were coming.'

'Maybe he's gone walking,' Dron said.

Bella raised her brows. 'Walking? At sixty below zero?'

'I thought he'd got used to the cold by now,' said Dron. 'Or maybe he's still down the mine.'

'He never works at night,' McKenna said. 'He likes the old ways. Days for work and nights for sleep. And why should he work nights anyway? The robot was programmed for that.'

The dome was warm. They took off their tunics. There must be an answer. Maybe Ben had found a new seam of gold. He always said there was more gold to be found in Oron.

Or maybe he was having fun. Teaching the robot more of those old Earth nursery rhymes he was so fond of. He'd begun to think of the robot as human. He'd even given it a name – Golar.

'There's nothing we can do now,' McKenna said. 'We'll get something to eat, then turn in. If Ben's in the mine, we'll find him in the morning.'

Next day they waited until the sun had driven away the cold. As McKenna pulled on his tunic, Bella had an idea. 'Did Ben make notes?'

'You mean on paper. Like the old days?'

'He was an old man,' Bella said. 'Set in his ways. Or maybe he left something on the screen. I think we should take a look. It might tell us where he is.'

There was no clue in Ben's rooms. Nor the store. Then Dron found something.

3

The old miner's day to day life flashed on the screen. His thoughts. Talk of Earth. The robot came up a lot. 'Gave Golar a rest' 'Taught Golar a new rhyme' 'Golar's a real friend . . .'

McKenna shook his head. 'Golar's been around too long. Ben needs a real friend, not that heap of rust. I told him last time to take a holiday back on Earth. He wouldn't listen. He . . .'

Dron cut in: 'See how often he talks about quakes, too, Captain? Look. Here. And here again. We know Oron's a bit unstable. But not like this. It seems things have got bad since we were last here.'

'It still doesn't tell us where Ben is. Let's speed things up. Bring up the last entry. There might be something there.'

Dron brought up Ben's last words: 'Earthdate 2502. Day 158. Big quakes. Went to mine. Roof came down on Golar. Did quick mend, but my friend is not his real self. Too many rhymes. Hope McKenna's got spares. Poor Golar. We'll soon put you right . . .'

'Poor Golar?' whispered Bella. 'Anyone would think that robot was flesh and blood.'

McKenna shook his head. 'To Ben, I think it is.'

The sun was strong now. As it rose above the peaks, McKenna and Bella pulled on their tunics. McKenna turned to Dron. 'Stay here. We'll stay in contact. If Ben turns up, beam me. If we find him, we'll beam you.'

The Korak nodded. Bella and McKenna went out. Dron watched them pass from view behind a fuel tank. Soon they reached a hill of newly-dug rock. It was low grade. Hardly worth mining. Hardly worth loading onto the ship. But Bella was not looking at the rock. She was looking at a man lying in deep shadow by the mine entrance.

They ran over to him. He was cut and battered. His eyes gazed at the pink sky but saw nothing. Ben was dead. McKenna reached down and took an old laser pistol from the dead hand. He saw a small mark on the side of the miner's head. 'He – he couldn't have,' mumbled McKenna.

But what else could he think? An old man stuck on a strange planet? With nothing but a robot for company? Being alone could do odd things to a man's mind. Ben had kept the laser since his days with the Space Unit. He must have used it one last time. On himself.

11

McKenna relayed Dron. 'We found him. We'll tell you the story later. We're going to look around the mine before we come back. If the robot's still working, I'll turn off its power. There's no more work to do here now.'

4

Rocks glowed in their head beams. The going was hard. The rubbish from 30 years mining lay across the ground. An old power line. The drill from some forgotten robot. A mug.

McKenna held up his arm. They listened hard. A faint noise came down the tunnel. It grew louder as they walked. It came from deep inside the mine.

'Ben's pal Golar?' said Bella.

McKenna nodded. It was Ben's robot, all right. Programmed to dig for gold until it burnt itself out. Two hours or 20 years. Ben or no Ben.

They reached a cavern. A dusky pink light fell around them. Tunnels led off. The noise came from one of the tunnels. Now it was an ear-splitting roar.

They came across Golar suddenly. Bella gulped. She'd never seen the robot before. It towered over her like a huge black shadow. She clutched at McKenna's arm. She felt as if every drill ever made was crashing through her brain.

Suddenly the noise stopped. The robot slowly turned from the rocks it had been drilling. Bella had her hands to her ears, and didn't hear the robot's syntha-voice. When she pulled them away, the voice sent shivers down her spine. It was evil. A harsh whisper. And above the mouth-slit red sensors glowed.

She felt as if she was looking into the eyes of the devil.

'Drilling ended. I wait for your next request, Captain McKenna,' Golar was hissing.

'No request. An order,' snapped McKenna. 'You do no more drilling. The mine is closed. Now.'

'Ben ordered me to dig.'

'Ben is dead.'

'I am not programmed to know 'dead' Captain McKenna. What is 'dead'?

'Have you ever had your microchips ripped out? That's dead. Now check out the rest of the gear. We're leaving Oron before night. With or without you.'

'I shall go in the dome with Ben.'

'Listen, you rust-heap. Ben's dead. DEAD. Got it? Now get to the shed. We'll be along when we've finished here.'

The robot pulled in its drill and began to glide towards the cavern. Bella turned to say something to McKenna when a small rock landed at her feet. The ground began to shake. Dust filled the air like fog. They began to cough. McKenna felt for the walls in the darkness. He remembered Ben's log: 'Big quakes, roof down . . .'

At last the thunder of the quakes rolled away. 'It's easing,' said McKenna. 'When the dust's clear we'll get out of here. Fast.'

They moved slowly towards the cavern. The clouds began to settle. But their way was blocked. Golar stood there. It nearly filled the tunnel. Its eye-sensors blazed. And its drill was slowly turning.

5

The robot rolled slowly towards them. Its drill whirred softly.

'I told you to get back to the shed,' snapped McKenna.

The robot came closer. For the first time Bella saw a worried look on McKenna's face. And his hand was on Ben's laser-pistol. A stride away Golar stopped.

'I am not programmed to know dead. Not dead not . . . not understand dead . . . not dead Captain.'

'What's the matter with it?' Bella asked.

'Its chips have packed in,' McKenna answered. 'Listen, you junk box. One more step and I'll blast you.'

'I am going to the shed now, Captain McKenna.'

'Make sure you do.'

The robot moved off, then turned. A ray-tube slowly came out from between its red sensors. It was pointing at the two figures by the tunnel wall.

'My ray is pointing . . . pointing at you Captain. I am programmed to dig ore dig ore . . . I dig dig dig dig dig dig dig and work the whole day through . . .'

'What's it singing?' whispered Bella.

'Some old song it's picked up from Ben.' McKenna raised his voice. 'Take in your tube. Put in the tube or I'll blast your sensors.'

The robot began to sing. 'Little Jack Horner sat in a corner eating . . . Christmas . . . spider sat down beside her and . . . dig dig dig the whole day through.'

'It's flipped,' said McKenna, aiming the laser.

'Must be the quakes,' Bella said. 'Ben taught it the rhymes. But like it said in his log, the roof came down on it.'

The robot's drill stopped. Golar was still for a moment. Its ray-tube was still pointing at them. Bella nudged McKenna. 'Why is it fitted with a ray-tube? There's nothing to kill on Oron.'

'The robot was shipped here from Bora, way back. There were riots there. It needed the tube. It –'

A sting of light left the robot's tube and hit the wall at McKenna's side. He threw himself down and squeezed Ben's laser pistol. Nothing happened. Another pulse struck a rock above. It crashed hard by McKenna's head. He sprang away. 'The laser's had it. Get back!'

They flung themselves into the tunnel as Golar came towards them. Its syntha-voice echoed against the rock. 'The owl and the pussycat went to sea in a beautiful pea-green boat. They took some honey and plenty of money wrapped up in a £5 note. I dig dig dig ore dead dead.'

Bella was close to tears. From far away came another rumble. McKenna glanced back. Golar was drilling again. It seemed to have forgotten them. McKenna took his relay from his belt and flicked it on. 'Dron,' he whispered. 'This is McKenna . . .'

Dron was only half-awake when the call came through. He coiled three green fingers around his relay and put it to his mouth. The voice he heard was a dull crackle. 'Dron, we've got problems. The robot's out of control. Here's what you do. Don't come in after us. The mine is likely to cave in any time. If we're not out of here before late-sun, take the pod. And get back to the ship. Fast.'

'But, Captain –'

'Don't enter the mine. That's an order. Over and out.'

Dron sat thinking for a time. Then he pulled on his tunic and went out.

6

Back in the tunnel, Bella was shaking with fear. McKenna lay in a hollow close by. The robot's drill crashed through the tunnel.

'Can't we do anything?' Bella pleaded.

'There's no point in giving any more orders,' McKenna hissed. 'Its sensors have crashed.'

'We've got to get out. Is there no way?'

McKenna drew a long breath. 'Behind it's a dead end. It's just a long shot, but –'

'But what?'

'Maybe we can sneak past it while it's drilling. Then we can make a run for it before the roof caves in.' Another rumble shook the air. It was louder this time. 'When I give the word – run like hell. Ready? Go!'

He gripped her hand and they ran together. They'd covered more than half the ground when the drill stopped. McKenna was a stride from Golar's tube before he stopped.

He saw a pulse of light. A sudden pain. Then blackness . . .

When he came to, McKenna found himself slumped on the ground. His head beam lay in bits by his side. Bella was dabbing at a gash above his ear.

'What happened?'

'You were hit.'

He lifted himself up and rubbed his shoulder. 'It must be set on 'stun'.' The robot was a little way off. It was still again, as if its cells had run dry.

Bella whispered: 'Do you want to make another run for it?'

McKenna was about to nod when a sound like the wing beat of an insect came from the robot. 'Little Jack Horner Horner sat . . . sat in in in his corner eats pie pie pie . . . Next time I will not miss, Captain McKenna. Next time I shall destroy you.'

'Shut up!' screamed Bella. 'Shut up!'

She fell, sobbing at McKenna's side. Golar was still. It fixed them with its dull red sensors. 'What are you?' she screamed. 'The devil? If you're going to end it, why not do it now? What are you waiting for?'

The robot put out its tube. The tube was pointing again at McKenna's head. 'You were right. My tube was set to stun, Captain,' it rasped. 'Now I have changed the setting. I will destroy you very soon.'

'It can't re-set its own tube, can it?' asked Bella.

'It may be a lie,' McKenna answered. Even he had begun to think the robot was human.

'I do not know lie, Captain. What is lie?'

McKenna turned to Bella. 'I told Ben never to mess with the robot's chips,' he hissed. 'If he's messed with the robot's tube, we're —'

Golar moved nearer. The tube was nearly touching McKenna's head. 'At one time Earth people did a countdown before a rocket's exit into space. I intend to do the same before your exit, Captain. 10 9 8 . . .

McKenna waited for the blast. There was nothing more he could do.

* * *

Dron ran through the first of the tunnels. His eyes grew wide as they got used to the pale underground light. Like all Koraks, his green eyes were as good in darkness as in daylight. He'd chosen to ignore McKenna's order. He'd turned off his relay so no more commands could reach him.

As he got to the cavern, a sudden tremor brought him down. A roar like a hundred Korak war drums shook the air. The tunnel seemed to tilt. His six green fingers gripped the walls.

The quake rumbled into silence. Dron lay on the ground. His relay was still in his belt. He took it out. 'Captain McKenna. Over.'

There was no reply. Dron rose slowly to his feet. 'Captain McKenna. Come in.'

He heard the far-off sound of rocks falling. He felt a shock of loneliness. Bella and McKenna. They'd meant more to him than his so-called friends on Korak. What had happened to them? He sat on a rock to think. After a time he heard a buzzing noise. It sounded like a drill. It echoed down the tunnel.

Then he heard something else. A voice singing. One of the old Earth songs Ben used to sing. 'The grand old Duke of York, he had 10,000 men . . .'

Dron stood up. Slowly, he made his way towards the sound.

7

Bella choked and opened her eyes. Her headbeam had gone out. Clouds of dust hung in the air. She pulled her emergency tank from her hip and took a lungful of clean air.

She felt better right away. But where was McKenna? The tunnel was silent now. She felt a trickle of blood on her hand. She tried to keep back the tears. 'McKenna, where are you?'

There was no reply. She sank to the floor. In her dazed state she could hardly feel the velon under her fingers. Velon. Space tunics were made of it! McKenna!

At first she could see nothing in the dusty air. Then she found an arm-pocket where he kept his beam. She took it out and flicked the switch. A strong light cut through the dust. In it, she saw McKenna's lifeless form.

She took a bottle of Revite from his backpack and gave him a shot in the arm. He didn't move. Then a weak groan came from his throat. At the same time his eyes blinked open.

'It's all right,' she told him. 'There's been a roof-fall.'

'My leg . . . Golar . . .'

His eyes rolled in the beam. Bella bent over him. She tried to make him understand. 'There was another quake. Your leg's trapped. My relay's smashed. And my headbeam. We're lucky to be alive.'

McKenna tried to get up. A stab of pain shot through his leg. Bella put a hand on his shoulder. 'Wait till the Revite works. No need to hurry.'

'What happened to the robot?'

'It's all right. Golar's gone.'

'Gone where?'

'I think the roof came down on it.'

McKenna grew stronger. He sat up. 'So where's the way out?'

Bella turned away. She didn't know the answer. She tried to sound bright. McKenna saw her smile fade. He began to tug at his leg. Bella bent down. She helped move away a big stone.

25

His leg was trapped under some rocks.

'Well?' he rasped.

'I think its okay. Just trapped.'

'It doesn't feel just trapped. It feels just broken.'

She worked at the rock jamming his leg. Suddenly, it was free. McKenna lay back. Beads of sweat had broken out on his face. Bella looked at his leg in the light of the beam. His knee was cut and swelling like a balloon. She asked: 'Can you walk?'

He gave a short laugh. 'Walk where? The roof's down. And this tunnel's our only way out.'

8

Dron listened. He could still hear the voice through a blanket of dust. He put his hand to his hip. But he'd left his laser on the ship. There had never been anything on Oron to shoot at.

He felt worried. What was McKenna's last relay? Had the robot gone mad? Maybe he should have stayed in the dome like McKenna said. It was too late now. He had to see what had happened to him and Bella. He was sure they were in trouble.

He moved forward again. Suddenly, he saw Golar. The robot was still in the tunnel. Only its drill was turning. Dron hid behind a rock and waited. The robot's syntha-voice clicked and it began to speak.

'My heat sensor tells me someone is there. It is Dron. The Captain's friend. I am programmed to see heat-fields. Your heat-field is low. So you are a Korak. The only Korak who comes to Oron is Dron. So you are Dron.'

Nothing seemed to be wrong with the robot. Yet a moment ago it had been singing Earth songs. Dron decided to show himself. 'Where is McKenna and the girl?' he asked.

'I do not know. I do not know about them.'

'Where were they when you last saw them?'

'I am not programmed to know dead. Ben fixed me up. He told me Earth songs. He called them Nursery Rhymes. I sing them when I work. Shall I sing you a Nursery Rhyme?'

'Not now.'

'I used to sing to Ben. He taught me to sing many songs. You are Dron. Dron the Korak. Little Bo-Peep has lost her sheep and doesn't know where to find them . . .'

There was evil in the robot's syntha-voice. Something was wrong. Dron stepped back. As he did, Golar came towards him fast. Now the robot towered above him like a black knight from the old Earth stories. Dron saw with a shock that its tube was pointing at him.

'What are you doing with a ray-tube?'

'I am going to destroy you. When I have destroyed you I shall dig gold dig dig gold. Destroy you and dig dig dig.'

A shiver ran down Dron's green back. His only chance was to play for time. And hope the robot would right itself to give him time to get back.

'And why do you want to kill me?'

'I do not understand, Dron. Tell me what you mean.'

'Have you killed the Captain?'

'I do not know kill. I know destroy. I destroy rock. I was programmed to destroy the Borans before I came here. Then my program was changed. I was set to dig gold. My tube was turned off. But Ben fixed me up. He changed me again. Now my tube works well. Now I can destroy anything. I will destroy you.'

Dron took a step back. The tunnel began to shake. He fell to the floor . . .

In another part of the mine, McKenna shook his head. 'It's hopeless,' he told Bella. 'The tunnel's jammed up.'

'There must be a way. There has to be.' She lifted a hand to her cheek. 'Can you feel cold air from somewhere?'

He propped himself up. He gave a grunt of pain. 'Yes. There is something. Back there.'

She aimed the beam down the tunnel. It looked like a dead end. She gave McKenna a hand up. They began to walk slowly down the passage. The beam picked up a wall of solid rock. McKenna shook his head. 'I never thought I'd die here. Ten light years from my own galaxy.'

The ground began to shake again. 'Maybe the robot's got it right,' went on McKenna. 'Maybe we should try singing those old Earth rhymes. To keep our spirits up. How do they go? Little Jack Horner, sat in –'

Bella's voice was like a whip crack. 'Captain! Come here!'

McKenna saw a thin crack in the rock. It ran from roof to ground. He held his hand to it and felt cold air. 'It can't be far to the other side,' he said to himself.

He was wondering how to open out the gap when the same quake that bowled Dron off his feet came down the tunnel. Rocks fell from the roof. They waited for the dust to clear. Bella put her beam by a stone and gulped more air from her tank.

The dust began to settle. She shone the beam. Where there had been rock was now open space. 'The quake's brought the walls down,' she gasped.

McKenna looked up. 'I think we've found our way out,' he said.

9

Dron lay still. The robot's drill spun in the dusty air. Its tube still pointed at him. Golar did not fire. From its syntha-voice came bits of old songs.

As the Korak waited, his hand closed on some chunks of rock. Fixing his eyes on Golar, he played for time. 'And when will you destroy me? Now? Tomorrow? Make sure you set the tube right.'

'I will destroy you, Dron. My ray-tube is set. It will destroy you easily.'

'Maybe I'm too strong to destroy. I'm not like the Borans, you know. They have the body of an Earth insect. You could destroy them on 'stun'.

The drill was spinning faster now. The tube moved from side to side. Dron gripped the stones in his green fingers.

'I will destroy you, Dron. Korak Dron.'

'Why me? The roof-fall must have crushed you. It must have messed up your chips. Ben did a bad job on you. Now you are mad, Golar. That's what I think.'

'Mad? What is 'mad'? Jack Sprat could eat no fat his wife could eat no lean.'

'Rhymes, Golar. Silly rhymes spoken by little children 1,000 years ago. Another time. Another galaxy. You don't even know what they mean. Who was Jack Sprat? Why wouldn't he eat fat? What's a wife? Could you destroy Jack's wife?'

A whine came from the drill. It was spinning fast. A pulse of light clipped the side of Dron's boot. The robot's sensors flamed like fire. 'I do not understand,' it screamed. 'Do not understand. Not understand. Not under. Dig gold. Dig dig Dron –'

The sensor darted here and there. The ray tube twisted and jerked. The drill screamed. Dron saw his chance. He threw the rocks into Golar's evil eyes. The sensors cracked. The robot began to spin.

'I cannot see. Where are you, Dron? I cannot see where are you Dron? I cannotsee. Whereareyou Dron . . .'

Bursts of laser light struck the tunnel. They flung rocks into the air. Then the robot stopped. Its tube was still. No words came from its syntha-voice. A quiet settled in the passage.

The sensors in the robot's head began to shatter. A million red bits fell to the ground. There were holes where the sensors had been. From the holes oozed a thick green liquid.

'What now, Golar?' cried Dron. 'Your sensors have gone. Your cells are dying. Who will you destroy now?'

In a low voice the robot began to sing. 'Hey diddle diddle the cat and the fiddle the cow jumped . . . over . . . the . . . moon.'

The voice faded. The robot did not move. Dron began to edge back to the entrance. His eyes never left Golar's silent form . . .

As Dron was making his escape, Bella stepped into the gap where the end of the tunnel had been. McKenna followed. The tunnel walls had been ripped apart by the quake. As they climbed over fallen rocks they heard more far-off rumbles.

'We'd better be quick,' urged Bella. 'This place could fall in at any time.'

'The air's getting colder,' McKenna said. 'Bring the beam up.'

Bella shone the light above McKenna's head. They looked up. And gasped. Lost for words. 'It's . . . it's . . .' McKenna began.

'Is 'wonderful' the word you're looking for, Captain?' Bella smiled.

10

The robot suddenly moved. It lifted its tube. Dron had moved ten steps back before the robot spoke. 'I will destroy you, Dron,' it whispered. Dron gave no answer.

'I cannot see, Dron. I have no seeing sensors. My cells are going. But my heat sensor is working, Dron. I will find you with my heat sensor. And I will destroy you as I destroyed the Borans before I came to Oron.'

The robot began to glide towards the green shape of Dron. 'I know you are here, Korak. I can feel your heat in the dark. I will find you.'

It crashed into the walls as it came towards him. For a moment he stopped. Then he raced for the exit as fast as he could go . . .

Meanwhile, two black specks were gazing upwards. The cavern was so big their beam couldn't reach the roof. But it reached the gold. Gold that gleamed from the rock. Gold that glinted in thick bands. More gold than they'd ever seen before.

McKenna spoke. 'So Ben was right after all,' he whispered. 'He always said there was more gold on

Oron. There's enough here to keep us going for a hundred years. I'll make another trip. Maybe I'll get a new ship. More crew.'

Bella said: 'First, we have to get out.'

They moved on, going by the feel of fresh air. Then there was a glimpse of the pink Oron sky. They'd come out on a ledge high on the hillside. Some way off lay Ben's dome and the sheds.

'We made it,' McKenna grinned. 'Let's go and tell Dron what we found.'

It was after mid-sun when they reached the track. Oron was cooling. They had to reach Ben's place before it became a frozen world.

They were near to a group of sheds when another tremble ran through the ground. 'Maybe you should forget the gold,' Bella said. 'I don't think you'll get the chance to mine it –'

Her words were cut off by a faint noise from the sheds. A bird-like sound. Bella reached for McKenna's arm. 'Golar!' she whispered. 'I thought it had got buried!'

'The rock must have fallen between it and us,' McKenna said. 'Did Dron have a blaster?'

'Bella gave a bitter laugh. 'Of course he didn't. He even left his laser pistol behind, like the rest of us. We came to check out gold, not to fight a crazy robot.'

The ground shook again. A huge rock crashed from the hill onto the track. They ran fast for the dome. Dron had to be warned there was a mad robot on the loose. As the chill of late day swept from the hills, they reached Ben's home. A pale wash of light came from the window.

As McKenna reached the door, something made him turn. By the mine entrance he could just make out the dark shape of Golar. Something else. On the ground. Bella saw it too. 'I think we're too late,' she said.

* * *

The ground was trembling. If the Korak had not fallen he might have made it to the dome. He'd been well ahead of the robot when he tripped. He'd knocked himself out. When he came to he found Golar above him. More horror. For the first time he saw Ben. The old miner was lying a short way off. It was clear Ben was dead.

Dron raised his head. He saw Bella and the Captain about to go into Ben's dome. He tried to get up. But he couldn't make his legs work. 'So you won in the end,' he said, almost to himself. 'What now, Golar?'

The drill spun fast. Dron gazed at the holes where the robot's red eyes used to be. Golar was very near. 'Korak,' it was hissing. 'I will destroy you.'

11

More tremors ran through the air. The dome shook. An odd rushing noise swept across the dark Oron hills. Night was coming fast. Flashes of red and blue light came from gashes that had opened in the cliffs.

Oron was waking. Fires which had burnt deep under the ground had broken out. The planet of gold was breaking up.

McKenna forced open the dome door. Inside, Dron's cup rolled across the floor. Ben's old compass had broken up. Sheets of paper lay everywhere.

McKenna kicked aside the cup and sat at the controls. The lights went out. The dome's wires began to fizz. 'Bella. Get me a bar. Something I can jam in this cabinet.'

'But shouldn't we – '

'Don't argue!'

The dome's sides were starting to crack. Ribbons of power jumped between the cells and snaked along the floor. A control box burst into flames. Bella found what she was looking for. McKenna grabbed it from her and jammed it in the cabinet.

'What're you doing? Let's go now before the whole thing breaks up!'

'There's time,' snapped the Captain.

'Time for what? No one can open that cabinet but Ben. It needs his hand print on the key pad. Why do you want to open it? Leave it and run.'

'It's starting to open,' grunted McKenna.

'I'm going back to the pod,' screamed Bella. 'I'm getting the hell out!'

With a crack the cabinet door gave way. It was open at last. 'I'm going nowhere without Dron,' yelled McKenna. 'And unless I blast that robot, Dron will be with Ben in miners' heaven.'

* * *

Dron was sure he was going to die. He didn't blame the robot. It was a machine. It had gone wrong. Ben had fixed it and made mistakes. It had drilled gold. Now it was going to drill the Korak. Or blast him with its ray-tube.

He looked again at Ben, lying there. Then he looked up at the robot. 'There's someone else here, Golar,' he heard himself say. 'Ben's here. Your friend. He teaches you to say the rhymes. Remember?'

The robot was still. Its drilling turned softly. It seemed to be listening.

'You haven't forgotten Ben, have you? He fixed you up. He looked after you. You were friends. Buddies. You dug gold together. Years of digging gold.'

'Ben.' The syntha-voice was low. 'I know Ben. Is he here?'

'Just here. In this shadow. I think he is resting. He might be hurt. I will take you to him. You can follow me. Use your heat sensors.'

'I will follow you, Korak. I will go to Ben. Ben is my friend. Ben is part of me.'

Dron moved slowly to where the dead miner lay. The robot came up behind. It came up against Ben's body. The drill was still. It felt Ben's body with the drill.

'Ben. You are here. I've been looking for you. I have been looking for you in the mine. Why don't you answer, my friend? Shall we sing some songs together?'

As the robot stood over the dead miner, Dron saw his chance. With a sudden leap he ran towards the dome as fast as his legs would take him.

He was sure the robot would fire. He'd feel the sting of the laser. Any moment he might die. He reached the door and hit it hard with his fist. McKenna flung it open. The Korak fell inside.

Bella and McKenna helped him to his feet. The three of them stood in the shaking dome.

'Better get to the pod fast,' Bella yelled.

'Not till I've put paid to the robot,' McKenna shouted back.

His fingers were playing with the buttons in the cabinet when there was a crash. The door flew open. Golar stood there. Only it was not Golar. It was Ben. Ben's head on Golar's steel body.

Bella let out a scream. McKenna took a step back. 'My God,' he whispered. 'It's taken Ben over. It wants his eyes. It thinks it's him.'

The ray-tube rose from the middle of Ben's head. A pulse of light took a chunk from the dome wall. McKenna was staring at the rows of buttons in the control panel. Another sting shot past his ear. There was a bigger button than the rest. A red button. In the corner. He closed his eyes and pressed it hard.

The dome seemed to grow quiet. He opened his eyes. The ray tube fell from Ben's face onto the ground. As they watched, the robot's hatch exploded. A green liquid seeped through cracks in Golar's metal body. Ben's head began to melt away.

'I did not know about Death. Death was not in my program. Now I understand. I am dying. Ben and I are dying together. Ben is here with me. He is my buddy. Will he stop me from dyinnnnnnnngggg?'

The robot's voice was one long wail.

'I know what a wife is now. It is a woman. Ben told me. Ben is here with me. Now. Inside my chips. Ben is my brain. Tell me the rhymes again. Shall we tell them, Ben? Yes. Ben says yes. We will sing a song together.'

'Jack Sprat could eat no fat, his wife could eat no lean –' McKenna stared. The voice was no longer a syntha-voice. It was Ben's. Ben's voice, getting slower, deeper, fading.

There was a smell of burning. Flames leapt from the hole where Ben's head had been. Now the voice was just a whisper in the Oron dusk.

12

The pod door slid aside. Bella thrust the pod forward along the track. Behind them the dome suddenly exploded. Showers of sparks filled the air.

As Bella drove, spears of light flashed from the mountains. A cloud of fire ran across the sky. In the distance they saw the ship. It stood like a black spider against the lights.

The pod skimmed the ground. Everything seemed to be moving. The Oron night rushed in on them. Freezing the water in their bodies. Turning their blood to ice.

'Run like hell for the ship!' shouted McKenna.

His beard became white as he hit the air. Dron was strong again. He almost lifted Bella from her feet. He struggled to give McKenna a hand up the ladder. They got into the ship and the door slid shut behind them.

'Strap in!' hissed the Captain. 'We're taking off!'

A roar of sound struck the ship from every side. It shook like a living thing. For a second it didn't seem as if they'd make it. Dron looked out of the port. His eyes were wide with shock.

'You won't see Oron again,' he said.

The planet was breaking up. Where the rocket had stood was a spinning pool of liquid gold.

* * *

The ship was warm. Slowly they drank their coffees and looked out into space. The stars gleamed.
A jagged light hung over Oron, now just a dot in the darkness.

Dron turned to face them. 'Thanks.'

'What for?'

'For saving us. I didn't know you could just push a button and destroy the robot.'

'That makes two of us,' McKenna said with a smile. 'It was just a long shot. For once Ben did the right thing.'

'You mean he –'

'Yes. He set the control so he could destroy Golar as well as the mine. Lucky I picked the right button. Pity he didn't have time to use it himself.'

'What d'you mean?' asked Bella.

'I thought you'd worked it out,' McKenna said. 'Ben didn't kill himself. It was Golar. The roof came down on it. Ben did a quick mend, but turned on Golar's anger sensors without knowing it. The robot shot Ben with the ray tube. Then he forgot about it and went back to dig gold.'

'And that's where we came in,' said Bella.

'Right. We found the old man at the foot of the cliff. He had his laser pistol, a keepsake from the old days. A bit of junk that didn't work.' He turned to Dron. 'All I have to say to you, my old Korak friend is . . . next time obey orders.'

Dron laughed. 'Ben always said there was more gold than you could dream of!'

'But how did the robot come to be Ben?' asked Bella. 'It was the most horrible thing I've ever seen.'

McKenna thought for a moment. 'Maybe there was more to those Boran machines than we knew. Maybe it turned human because it spent so long with Ben.'

Now all that remained of Oron were ribbons of golden flame.

There was a sudden flash of brilliant light. They shut their eyes. For a second the ship hung in white heat on the edge of space. When they next looked, Oron had gone.

'Our last trip to Oron,' Bella said.

They climbed into their bunks and slept. Although they didn't see it, a chunk of Oron had blasted through the blackness. Now it lay on a ledge below one of the ports.

It was a lump of pure gold.

If you enjoyed this story, why not try this other **NEW SPIRALS** science fiction story:

Spots by Bill Ridgway